To

_____

From

_____

Date

_____

A grandmother is
a little bit parent, a little bit teacher,
and a little bit best friend.

—Author Unknown

A Gift Book for Grandmas
and Those Who Wish to Celebrate Them

What If There Were No Grandmas?

Caron Chandler Loveless

Illustrations by Dennis Hill

HOWARD BOOKS
A DIVISION OF SIMON & SCHUSTER
New York   London   Toronto   Sydney

What if all grandmas
one day disappeared?
Their grandkids would wail,
"What is happening here?"

At first we might guess
they were just playing games.
We'd run through their houses
and shout out their names.

Hey, Nana! Granny! Mamaw! or Mimi!
Yo, Meemaw! Abuela! Nanny! and Gigi!

Who could imagine a scene such as this?
What grandma would leave without even a kiss?

Maybe, we'd think, they were all on a trip,
Off sailing the seas on a grandma cruise ship.
We'd all want to know:
what could be their intention?
Perhaps they've all gone to a grandma convention!

Having grandmothers gone
could become quite a problem.
The issues are endless:
just how would we solve them?
Right off the top there would be tons of trouble:
Like serving ice cream—who'd say, "Have a double!"?

No one would ask what you plan to be,
with a pat on the head like you were still three,

Then say, "My, you've grown,"
and "Aren't you so smart?"
And frame all your scribbles
like fine works of art.

Little things would get missed,
like a purse full of gum,
and Grandma's sweet voice,
asking, "Don't you want some?"

Just think of the smell from her kitchen at lunch,
and how she flipped pancakes
for the family brunch.

Kids wouldn't get cookies with sprinkles on top,
and homemade piecrust would roll to a stop.

Who'd tell you to keep good thoughts in your head?
Or teach you to sew with a needle and thread?

With no grandmas here, well,
some things we'd not see,
like plastic rain hats
and public TV.

Who'd shout, "That's the Beatles!
        That's Louis Armstrong!"
Then crank up the music
    and belt out a song?

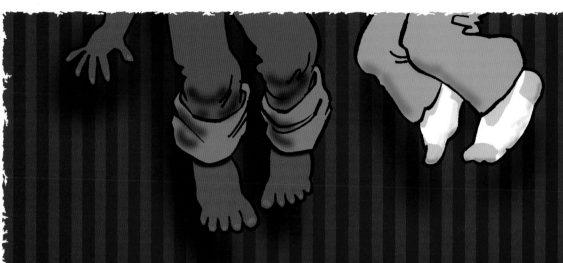

You'd not get permission to jump on the bed,
or slide down the staircase or paint your face red.

Who would save money to send us to college?
Or pass on her wisdom and limitless knowledge?

If grandmas were gone,
who would pinch, pat, and squeeze us?
Or hand us a tissue for each of our sneezes?

There'd be no reunions where relatives meet,

and all family trees would remain incomplete.

Who'd tuck you in bed under *her* grandma's quilt?
Or remember the year the old homestead was built?

Who'd say that our eyes
were passed down from her side?
Or show us old photos
of herself as a bride?

No grandma to point out the clouds in the sky,
and never get tired of hearing a "Why?"

Who'd never ignore you when you needed to speak?
But peck her pink lipstick right there on your cheek?

Who'd say with a wink
as she turned to go,
"You're my *favorite* grandchild,
I want you to know!"?

Now, a world without grandmas we just can't allow.
Let's give thanks for Grandma! Let's honor her now!

No, a world without grandmas we couldn't abide.
Let's celebrate Grandma! Rejoice far and wide!

So I jump to my feet,
and give out a shout,
to one that, for sure,
I can't do without.

My own precious _____ (grandma),
please never go far,
how cherished . . . how needed . . .
you certainly are!

So to you, Grandma, I just have to say . . .
Could I live without you?

Absolutely NO WAY!

Grandma, I couldn't live without you because:

_____

_____

_____

_____

_____

_____

_____

_____

_____

_____

Grandparents are proud of
their grandchildren.
—Proverb 17:6a

Our purpose at Howard Books is to:
• *Increase faith* in the hearts of growing Christians
• *Inspire holiness* in the lives of believers
• *Instill hope* in the hearts of struggling people everywhere
Because He's coming again!

Published by Howard Books, a division of Simon & Schuster, Inc.
1230 Avenue of the Americas, New York, NY 10020
www.howardpublishing.com

What If There Were No Grandmas? © 2008 by Caron Chandler Loveless

Library of Congress Cataloging-in-Publication Data

Loveless, Caron, 1955–
  What if there were no grandmas / Caron Loveless ; illustrated by Dennis Hill.
    p. cm.
  1. Grandmothers—Poetry. 2. Christian poetry. I. Hill, Dennis.
II. Title.
  PS3612.O838W46 2007
  811'.6—dc22
                              2007033651
ISBN-13: 978-1-4165-5196-6
ISBN-10:   1-4165-5196-4

10 9 8 7 6 5 4 3 2 1

Manufactured in China

For information regarding special discounts for bulk purchases, please contact: Simon & Schuster Special Sales at 1-800-456-6798 or business@simonandschuster.com.

Edited by Chrys Howard
Cover design by Stephanie D. Walker
Interior design by Dennis Hill and Stephanie D. Walker
Illustrations by Dennis Hill

Scripture quotations, unless otherwise marked, are taken from the Holy Bible, New International Version®. Copyright © 1973, 1978, 1984 by International Bible Society. Used by permission of Zondervan. All rights reserved.